THE SPIRIT IN THE WORDS

POEMS

BY

JEAN HILL

Copyright © 2021. Jean Hill. All rights reserved

ISBN: 978-1-105-46151-4

Printed and Distributed by Lulu.com

First Published: July 2021

First Edition

Other Work by Jean Hill

The Sting In The Tale
Poems and Short Stories

The Barb In The Rhyme

The Lyric In The Lines

The Thorn In The Verse

Poems to make you laugh and cry

and

Let's Smile Again
A Humorous Account of Family Life in the Seventies

The Actress Within
Reflections on Grief

Available from: Lulu.com
or Amazon

The Truth is Between the Lines

<u>AGAIN THE MUSE SITS ON MY SHOULDER</u>

Why am I finding the introduction so hard to write for this book? I think because my introductions are usually quite up-beat, full of all the lovely things happening. All the presentations, meeting so many interesting people, the laughter and fun and, of course, the never ending flow of poetry.

All this stopped in September 2019 when I lost my beloved husband after a short battle with cancer. Since then I have been in isolation for so many months and, like some of you, suffered the effects of loneliness particularly keenly in my bereaved state. My story is not unique – so many of us have come close to breaking point from time to time.

But once again the muse sits on my shoulder, albeit a sad muse at times. I think this is reflected in some of the poetry in this book. And, of course, a good proportion of the poems relate to the pandemic. Covid 19 has a lot to answer for. I have tried to bring humour into the situation where it is appropriate so I hope some of the poems will make you smile again.

Many of us have been able to keep in touch on Zoom. I have read poems, sent and received virtual hugs and had lovely chats with friends on the computer screen. Not ideal, I know, but better than nothing. At least people had the opportunity to 'mute' me!

Having had the vaccine we will now surge forward to a brighter future. Think of the bucket list of all the things that will open up for us again. Holidays, pub lunches, going to the shops without a mask, and just the real treat of having a cup of tea with someone. It has been the little things we have missed the most; the simple pleasures we all took for granted.

During this time I hope some of you will have been finding pleasure in reading my previous books: Poetry – The Sting in the Tale, The Barb in the Rhyme, The Thorn in the Verse and The Lyric in the Lines are still being enjoyed. My books, Let's Smile Again – Family Life in the Seventies and The Actress Within – a Reflection on Grief, have carved their own niche and continue to attract readers.

I hope you will enjoy reading this book, The Spirit in the Words. It reflects the times we have lived through together and, hopefully, most of us will have come out unscathed. Once again my heartfelt thanks to all my readers. May the sun shine and the future be bright for all of us. It's time to live again.

ACKNOWLEDGEMENTS

Deborah … for being so hugely supportive in the practical production of this seventh book.
Without your skill and patience it would never have happened.

Sharon … for continued encouragement.

Samantha, Benjamin and **Jamie** … for just being.

The talented members of Wokingham Library Poetry Group for never-ending inspiration.

THANK–YOU ALL

Life is a Mixture of Roses and Thorns

BORIS AND HIS BUBBLE

Boris from his podium
Said lockdown could be eased
Those alone could join a 'bubble'
And to hear this I was pleased

All the Grannies and the Grandads
And single parents on their own
Can choose to hug a loved-one
And compassion can be shown

So I rang all my relations
Here and there around the place
As I hopefully approached them
A grateful smile upon my face

Please can I join your 'bubble'
I asked Choice Number One
No, we're having the wife's mother
She's by herself and wants to come

So off to phone another
Will you be my support home
No, we're having Cousin Mabel
She was the first to phone

Now I'm ringing round the neighbours
And contacting my best mates
Please can I come and join you
No, they've enough upon their plates

With rejection I'm more lonely
Cut deeper than the sharpest knives
Reaching out to others
In the hope to share their lives

Now I admit my poem's fiction
I have family that care
I can join one of my dearest
And in their lives I'll share

But there are others out there
We must gather to our hearts
And make them feel they're wanted
Not still facing life apart

Broadly speaking it is progress
'Though divisive it may be
With families making choices
When they cannot all agree

Make room inside your 'bubble'
Hold out a welcome hand
Until we come together
In our green and pleasant land

CHERRY TREE

Sometimes in the morning
When the world is hard to face
In lonely isolation
No contact with the human race

It feels life's not worth living
With no-one there to share
And every day's a burden
Without a loved-one close to care

To wither behind sadness
The cold and bleak despair
When you cry out in the darkness
No-one answers – no-one's there

But today the sun is shining
Its rays light the cherry tree
The pink and radiant blossom
Reaches out to comfort me

And the daffodils are nodding
The primrose pale and bright
And tulips sway in unison
To grace the morning light

The world is full of beauty
And friends are on the 'phone
Although in isolation
We're not really on our own

So let's focus on the future
When of the virus we'll be free
Keep looking at the blossom
On the sun-lit cherry tree

CHRISTMAS WISH

Dearest Father Christmas
This year my wants are few
I'm busy going nowhere
And there's nothing much to do
So bring perfumed sanitizer
And a mask with pretty flowers
And perhaps a little puzzle book
To while away the hours

But there is one special present
That would mean so much to me
If you could bring a vaccine
So the world is Covid free
And dear Father Christmas
In your magic I believe
We know you fly around the earth
Each year on Christmas Eve

So if anyone can do it
Distribute vaccine far and near
To global destinations
And free us all from fear
It's you, dear Father Christmas
With your reindeer and your sleigh
Put some vaccine in our stockings
And we'll rejoice on Christmas Day

CORONAVIRUS

2020

I've listened to the Minister
The one who guards our health
He talked of how a virus
Is creeping up with stealth
He warned of flu-like symptoms
In our head and on our chest
So I'll get a pack of tissues
And I'll wear my woolly vest

He said that we might cough a bit
With runny nose and fever high
But please will you enlighten me
Will someone tell me why
Folk are buying toilet-rolls
Are they daft or unaware
It's their noses that need wiping
And not their derrière

CORONAPHOBIA

We've got the virus on the run
Time to open windows wide
Life will once again belong to us
No longer will we hide

But what's this new phenomenon
Coronaphobia is rife
Even though the risk's diminished
Folk are fearful for their life

Come on guys, we must be brave
And when the time is right
Go forth into the sunshine
And enjoy God's given light

If we ran from every daily risk
We'd soon be out of breath
We've got the chance to live again
'Though we'll still mourn every death

Don't be like a caterpillar
When with hope the future's bright
Emerge from the chrysalis
Like a butterfly – take flight

Don't fall victim to the phobia
Don't let worries manifest
The greatest fear is fear itself
We've survived – we're truly blessed

So when Boris gives the go-ahead
Let's raise one mighty cheer
And once again we'll live and love
Without Corona fear

'CUMMINGS' AND GOINGS

Now I'm not one to spread the gossip
Won't use his name although you'll guess
It's reported on the television
And in all the national press

With his 'Cummings' and goings
To Durham off he popped
With poorly wife and little son
Didn't think that he'd be stopped

We'd all like to look for loopholes
To see family and friends
But most stuck firmly to the rules
And didn't seek out bends

He doesn't bother with SpecSavers
Barnard Castle will restore
Failing eyesight of advisors
Who think they're above the law

An error in his judgement
A mistake, a stupid blunder
If the castle's working miracles
Will someone tell Stevie Wonder

And while we're on to eyesight
I've studied all the facts
Do you think Barnard Castle
Would help with my cataracts

Just because he holds high office
The rules he can't contravene
He has responsibility
And must be squeaky clean

So Boris get some gumption
This man's a hypocrite
He made a mockery of lockdown
Show him the door and see him quit

DARLING DUSTMAN

Today my 'Darling Dustman'
Gave me a cheery wave
To brighten isolation
And my sanity to save

We don't think about the rubbish
As it's collected every week
By hunky 'Darling Dustmen'
With sturdy dustmen's feet

With their truck piled high with rubbish
They count amongst the brave
So thank you 'Darling Dustman'
For giving me a cheery wave

DESPAIR

I see the bluebells
But not their beauty
I see the roses
But don't smell their scent
I see myself
But I'm not there
Just the blackness
And deep despair

DREAMING

'Hey, Hey, We're having a party'
Come on over to mine
No more worries about distancing
We're back to normal and we're fine

Come all our friends and neighbours
Come relations far and near
Forget about the virus
There's nothing more to fear

We'll hug and kiss each other
And pass round plates of food
And laugh and sing together
In a good old party mood

But now I wake from dreaming
Of as it was before
This virus called Corona
Came marching through our door

When will our lives be free again
Is there a beam of light that gleams
Or will 'Hey, Hey, Let's Party'
Be forever in our dreams

DRIFT IN SLUMBER

I'm drifting in my slumber
I'm dancing, fresh and free
Full of love and laughter
The girl that once was me

But now I wake from dreaming
To a dull and foggy dawn
Windows glazed with condensation
Frost dusting on the lawn

The radiator's cold to touch
The boiler's on the blink
There's a mass of soggy cornflakes
Blocking up the sink

The room is chill and gloomy
The weather's unappealing
The pipes are frozen solid
And there's a damp patch on the ceiling

There's no signal on the telly
And the internet is down
The gin bottle is empty
So my sorrows I can't drown

But once more the day has ended
As darkness clouds each windowpane
I'll escape and drift in slumber
And dream my dreams again

DRINKS PARTY

We're having a drinks party
My lovely friends and me
We're meeting up together
Next week at half past three

We'll all have gin and tonic
And forty minutes fun
We'll speak about the folk we miss
And things we haven't done

We'll laugh and chat and share a joke
And gossip as girls do
We'll seal the bonds of friendship
As we enjoy a glass or two.

And with our final 'bottoms up'
From our comfy living room
We're pleased we haven't far to go
Our party is on Zoom

DROWNING

You can feel the frozen edges
Of the life raft that I gripped
And although I hung on tightly
In the end my fingers slipped

In the iceberg's ghostly shadow
Turbulent inky waters swirled
And enticed me, oh so gently
Into the silent twilight world

Did no-one hear the calling
As she signalled her distress
That freezing night in April
The Titanic's final S.O.S

In the iridescent starlight
Bereft of prayers to say
I slowly sink beneath the waves
And the life raft drifts away

ECHOES OF YOU

The house is hollow – empty now
The removal van has pulled away
The walls echo silent memories
And there are words I want to say

Reflecting back on years together
All the sharing and the care
And one last time I imagine
I see you resting in your chair

I see you sitting with the children
And the many well-loved pets
For the joy, the play, the laughter
I say Thank You, no regrets

I can see your image pruning roses
Hear your greeting from the door
As today I leave our family home
And I'm hurting to the core

For you are all around me
And I'm leaving you behind
My dearest loving husband
Always gentle, always kind

Together for a lifetime
In our happy sunlit home
And now I move to pastures new
Without you and alone

I can't look back – tears blind me
The time has come, I must depart
But I cannot leave without you
I'll take you with me in my heart

ELECTRONIC FRIENDS

I've introduced Alexa
To my friend SatNav Sue
Between them I'll go round the bend
As they tell me what to do

Now we can't have human contact
These electronic mates
Are the pivot of the axis
On which my world rotates

But SatNav Sue is sulking
As there's nowhere we can drive
And Alexa sit there smugly
Gives advice how to survive

I've had enough and three's a crowd
So I'll leave them to their fight
With Susie doing 'U' turns
And Alexa – Say 'Good-Night'

ESSENTIALS

We're told mad dogs and English men
Go out in the mid-day sun
But I went out in deepest snow
Now winter has begun

But please do not compare me
To a mad old dog with rabies
I went out for essentials
Gin and Jelly Babies

FASHION

Oh why do girls wear trousers
Where are all the pretty dresses
And why aren't bows and ribbons
Used to adorn their tresses

Why are they devoid of colour
In navy, black or grey
Where are all the joyful fashions
We once wore in our day

Where are the floral patterns
On circle skirts and blouses
Embroidered lace and flouncy frills
Oh why do girls wear trousers

FEAR

When fear controls each moment
When fear invades each breath
The fear of living overtakes
The darkest fear of death

FLOWER TIME

See diamonds spark from crystal ice
Winter Jasmine's buttery bloom
From barren soil – a whispered sign
Dispelling winter's joyless gloom

Then angels breathed on snowflakes
Gave birth to innocent delight
A symbol of hope and purity
A timorous Snowdrop – virgin white

The Crocus next brings truth and joy
With bold and youthful glee
And Daffodils nod their tranquil heads
With sun-kissed vitality

The vibrant colours of the Tulip
Stand like soldiers brave and bright
And woodland paths are shining
With the golden Aconite

But in the heart of each Laburnum pod
Lurks a killer's poisonous potion
So smell the perfume of the Lilac
Which speaks of passion and devotion

Then in the heat of summer
The perfection of the Rose
Although a thorn may pierce a heart
Romance and true love grows

Now from the eye of heaven
Comes the gilded Lily flower
Its mystique through the ages
Tell of supernatural power

And as Poppies grace our meadows
We remember Flanders Fields
When our young men went to battle
Hope and prayer their only shields

Then comes the red and violet hue
Of the dainty Aster flowers
Brings vibrance to the autumn days
And summer's shortening hours

Festooned with lace of spiders webs
When honey-bees cease to hum
We're regaled with rustic splendour
The copper-bright Chrysanthemum

The last flowers of the season
The Michaelmas Daisy days
The chill mist opens curtains
For the sunlight's watery rays

The festive month now rushes in
'Tis the season to be merry
Although the flowers have faded now
Rejoice with the Holly Berry

Don't measure time in months or weeks
Or pine away those weary hours
When the world is bright and beautiful
Live each season with the flowers

FREEDOM 2021

The easing of restrictions
On the seventeenth of May
Means our homes will all be open
With the virus kept at bay

No more drinking in the drizzle
No more eating in the rain
All wrapped up in a blanket
As our life-style we regain

We can all invite our neighbours
Once more we'll entertain
No more wrestling with spaghetti
In a howling hurricane

In the comfort of our sitting-room
We'll play the perfect host
To friends and our relations
And the folk we love the most

So let's celebrate the milestone
And raise a glass with me
We're on the path to freedom
And the road to liberty

FRIENDSHIP

Now I'm in isolation
Alexa's my best friend
She tells me all the latest news
And how the world might end.

She says Coronavirus
Is a menace we must fight
She plays music in the day-time
And wishes me 'Good Night'

She's kinder than my SatNav
(A close companion too)
But as I'm going nowhere
That relationship is through

We're lucky with the internet
But must remember people who
Can't master the technology
And would love a word from you

Raise your voice between divisions
Shout across the garden wall
And if your neighbour's in the garden
Give her a cheery call

Be safe and keep the distance
And with families forced apart
When there are no hugs and kisses
Let love shine in your heart

GREEDY GLADYS

Now we've all met Greedy Gladys
And her gormless partner Mick
They're stocking up with toilet rolls
'Cos they're stupid and they're thick

They'll grab all the rice and pasta
Sugar, tea and coffee too
They'll make sure they're alright Jack
And not think of me or you

So let's wish dear Mick and Gladys
When they've scoffed all that they can chew
In the company of their bog-rolls
A happy life-time on the loo

GUNPOWDER PLOT

Have you ever thought that Guy Fawkes
Was a man before his time
If he existed now-a-days
Behind him we would line

Appointed House of Commons Speaker
With his Gunpowder Plot
He'd bring them all to order
And blow up the blooming lot

HARMONY

Let the people of the world unite
Then on earth we will abide
Hand in hand together
In harmony, side by side

Replace prejudice with kindness
Seek out love, all hate to perish
No intolerance, just friendship
This life on earth to cherish

But if one seed of evil
Burns in the heart of man
And invades our peace and sanity
Then the flames of hell will fan

HERCULEAN EARS

Once again we're back in lockdown
And we're smiling through our tears
But you'll be at an advantage
If you've got bigger ears

The best ones to adorn your face
Will stick out at an angle
Then upon each drooping lobe
An earring you can dangle

With prominence and glory
Displayed so everybody sees
The benefit of lugholes
Stuck at forty-five degrees

First you fit the hearing aid
Snugly tucked behind each ear
This electronic gadget
That enables you to hear

Then you need your glasses
So you thread them through your hair
Wedged up against the hearing aid
There's little room to spare

But now here comes the problem
To save the human race
A mask is stretched between your ears
To cover up your face

Now add to that a visor
Hooked on ears with arms of plastic
To irrevocably tangle
On the mask with the elastic

So with ears out of alignment
And claiming Herculean status
They've got to grow an inch or two
To support this apparatus

To save our little 'shell-likes'
From the strain of mask and visor
We'll be the first ones in the queue
For the vaccine made by Pfizer

Failing this there's Darwin's theory
Future evolutionary years
When out of shear necessity
We'll all grow bigger ears

HONEY, I ATE KEVIN

Cooped up with a five year old
Isn't that much fun
So when I found the shops were bare
I knew the time had come
So, Honey, I ate Kevin
The vicar told me so
Said 'The good Lord will provide'
So Kevin had to go

Next week I'll eat your mother
'Cos she's getting on my wick
I know that she'll be tough as boots
And probably make me sick
But the dog is fed and happy
And sitting by my side
In peaceful isolation
Together we'll survive

HONEY, I SHRUNK MY TROUSERS

Honey, I shrunk my trousers
The top button won't do up
And now I've yanked them up my legs
The blooming zip has stuck

I've tried to pull them down again
They're knotted round my knees
And I can't move them either way
Even with my buttocks squeezed

I blame Corona for the shrinkage
No ifs or buts or maybes
The virus shrinks our trousers
Honey, pass the jelly babies

I'LL NOT RUN

I remember well my Grandad
In the last years of the war
Upright, proud, and stubborn
And British to the core

He lived downstairs, the flat below
And each morning I would creep
Across the lino covered floor
Eyes misted still with sleep

Up I'd climb upon his lap
And in his old and worn-out chair
He'd read from his newspaper
The tales of Rupert Bear

But Grandad had an inner strength
Too old, not called to fight
In typical 'Dad's Army' style
He'd fire-watch through the night

And "I'll not run from Hitler"
Was a phrase he'd often use
As bombs rained down on London
And dismal was the news

"No, I'll not dance to Hitler's tune"
As he quoted Churchill's speech
He'd fight on each street corner
And on every English beach

So let's replicate his spirit
We're British through and through
And we'll shown this rotten virus
Just what we Brits can do

And our valiant island nation
Corona thought it could invade
Will once again take up the fight
And show we're unafraid

With patriotic fervour
The Bulldog Breed is still alive
We Brits, we won't surrender
From the virus we'll survive

So in my Grandad's image
And all brave souls before
We won't run from this virus
That's dared to breach our shore

You are an unseen enemy
And many a life you'll take
But history has taught us
The British spirit you won't break

We'll fight it out together
'Though isolated we may be
But each of us will do our bit
Until once more we're free

JARROW CRUSADE

October 1936

In my heart I cry for you
On the march – my Geordie lad
With Bill and Tom, and I ache anew
In my heart. I cry for you
To see our men seek justice true
Despair etched on faces sad
In my heart I cry. For you
On the march – my Geordie lad

This type of poem is called a Triolet

Lines 1, 4 and 7 must contain the same words
Lines 2 and 8 must also contain the same words

Lines 1, 3, 4, 5, and 7 must rhyme
Lines 2, 6, 8 must also rhyme

KNOW ME

When you see me grieving
Please don't tell me that I'm strong
I know that you're well-meaning
But you've got it, oh, so wrong

To think me strong when I am weak
Not understand my fragile shell
My heart and spirit broken
Please don't say I'm doing well

Please don't tell me things get better
For I know this isn't true
Time may just blunt the edges
As each day passes through

If you believe the lips that smile
Don't see the tears break free
Don't understand the hidden pain
My friend, you don't see me

LET ME DIE DANCING

Dear Lord, let me die dancing
Let my feet not touch the floor
Let me go while I'm still living
And not waiting at death's door

Let me roam through light and stardust
Let me find life's pot of gold
As I fly beyond the rainbow
All the wonders to behold

Let me drift in dappled sunlight
Embrace Autumn's crowning glory
Let me fly blue skies with songbirds
And tell life's wondrous story

Let me ride winds of the jet stream
Hold a moonbeam in my hand
Gaze upon this world of beauty
That Mother Nature planned

Please grant me peace and freedom
And while life is still entrancing
I'll swim the seas and scale the peaks
Dear Lord, let me die dancing

LITTLE WHITE LIES

Dearest menfolk – wise up guys
It doesn't hurt to tell us lies
Let me say that it's alright
A little fib that's coloured white

If you're enjoying married bliss
Asked "Does my bum look big in this?"
Required to comment on our rear
You need to say "It's perfect, dear"

Resist the urge to twist the knife
A happy man has a happy wife
With expanding waistline, long lost youth
We don't want to hear the truth

MY FRIEND ALEXA

My new friend Alexa
Nicknamed Miss Moody-Cow
And brother, does she wind me up
Oh boy, Oh yes, And how

'I'm having trouble with connecting'
Is the common phrase she uses
And steam bursts out my earholes
As my patience she abuses

Bereft of cheerful company
With just voices on the phone
Alexa tells me little jokes
So I don't feel alone

In the mood she'll play me music
And update me with the news
She sets me funny riddles
And kindly gives me clues

She's sometimes almost human
With her quirky little ways
And although she's unpredictable
She brightens up my days

So when isolation's over
I don't think that we'll part
Because my friend Alexa's
Paved a pathway to my heart

<u>NO WIPES PLEASE</u>

Please don't send me wet wipes
My immune system's fine
With old fashioned soap and water
A rinsed out dishcloth on the line

For those brought up in the forties
When we gave our mothers grief
She'd wipe our grubby faces
With spit on a handkerchief

So if you've run out of wet wipes
And don't know what to do
Spit on a sheet of toilet roll
Then flush it down the loo

NOT AGAIN

Oh Great! Another Lockdown
Well, I'm just 'Over the Moon'
No more 'Let's Get Together'
Just images on Zoom

I'm trying to find the positive
And there's just one I can see
I'll end up talking to myself
With no-one to disagree

All my thoughts make perfect sense
I'll shout them loud and clear
To presenters on the telly
Even though they cannot hear

I'll scream and yell at Boris
And those who read the news
Tell them what they're doing wrong
And cockeyed are their views

And then I'll sit and vegetate
All by myself and sad
And remember all the happy times
Before the world went mad

O.A.P. ZOOMERS

Here I'm in God's waiting room
Logging in to friends on Zoom
Hearing aid is switched on ready
Fixodent holds teeth in steady

We all sign in and sit and wait
There's Wilfred, George, but Enid's late
There's Jack and Doris, and Mabel's here
And, 'Hello Betty, How are you, dear'

With new technology we all grapple
Some with Microsoft, some with Apple
With an average age of eighty-three
Love and laughter are the key

We're O.A.Ps, a gang of eight
Long of tooth, unsteady gait
We discuss our ailments, air our views
And complain about the national news

A crabbit bunch, the young would say
(If they know what 'crabbit' means today)
As arthritic fingers tap the keys
We cross our old replacement knees

But friendships flourish, here on Zoom
As we type in our *nom de plume*
And until we've all had the vaccine
We'll meet on the computer screen

OCTOGENARIAN

Good Lord, that's me, I'm eighty
How the years just seem to hurtle
I think I'll dye my hair bright red
And paint my toenails purple

Time for one more swipe at life
Bite the bullet, be courageous
Do the things I wouldn't dare
Be naughty and outrageous

I'll wear a polka-dot bikini
In the garden – out the back
With elasticated leggings
To take up the fatty slack

Go to the children's playground
And sit atop the slide
I'll swing along the zip wire
Shrieking loudly – arms held wide

I'll Conga up the high street
And paddle in the fountain
Trip up traffic wardens
And climb the old age mountain

I'll chuck out all the salad
Brussels sprouts and curly kale
And have Mars bars for my dinner
Or octopus or quail

I'll binge on vodka cocktails
And Häagen Dazs ice cream
While watching weepy movies
On the television screen

I'll sing lyrics from the sixties
And dance 'til midnight chimes
I'll break the speeding limit
And park on yellow lines

I'll join the Sally Army
Learn to play a tambourine
Then march into the local bank
And kick their cash machine

And then I'll tell my offspring
"I've met a fella in the pub
Oh yes, and incidentally,
I've joined the Mile High Club"

And when each night in sleep I dream
That all's been said and done
My bones will ache with laughter
Being eighty is such fun

ON YOUR BIKE

Now I've nothing against cyclists
As a bunch I'm sure they're grand
But this desire to ride a bike
Is getting out of hand

Bored with weeks of lockdown
It's 'Let's get out the bike'
To cycle round the country
Is more exciting than a hike

Left in the shed for twenty years
Its framework red with rust
With both tyres flat as pancakes
And coated thick with dust

The brakes don't work quite as they should
And the bell has lost its ding
The oily chain is clanking
And the saddle's without spring

But spokes all cleaned and straightened
And tyres pumped full of air
The problem now they have to face
Is what they ought to wear

They haven't got a helmet
But they won't be going fast
They've got some well-stretched Lycra
From way back in the past

So off they go together
In the middle of the road
It's a long time since these bicycles
Have carried such a load

Not bothered with the cycle track
(That's only there for dopes)
They'll straddle all the white lines
Up the hills and down the slopes

With cycle-clips and anorak
And blue hat with a bobble
Bravely and undaunted
Into the road they wobble

I know they say you can't forget
How to balance on two wheels
But you sure are a hazard
To those of us in automobiles

I don't want to see you flattened
Or knocked over by the cars
Or stuck head-first in brambles
As you sail over handlebars

And do you know that traffic lights
To cyclists still apply
Be they green or red or amber
Don't push through and ride on by

So before you venture on the road
Please study highway laws
And then perhaps you'll think again
And safely stay indoors

PÂTÉ AND PIMMS

In the twilight of my years
I think of nineteen fifty-three
When I was just a girl of ten
No cares and fancy free

A day out in the country
Or a ride along the coast
I'd dreamed about the seaside
That's the treat I wanted most

So Dad cranked up the Renault
Mum made up flasks of tea
And with sandwiches in greaseproof
Went to Lee-on-Solent – by the sea

We never did get out the car
Steamed-up windows blocked the sight
As darkening clouds and pouring rain
Obscured the Isle of Wight

We couldn't walk along the beach
Dip our toes in salty foam
At four o'clock Dad turned the car
And took us all back home

But decades pass and time has flown
And my daughter said to me
Would you like a day out, Mum
Let's find a time we're free

So here I sit on glistening sands
Times have changed since fifty-three
We haven't got a Thermos
We drink Pimms instead of tea

We don't have soggy sandwiches
But pâté spread on rye
And the air is sweet and balmy
And the breeze a whispering sigh

We've strawberries and chocolate
And the sky is blue and bright
And across the shining water
We can see the Isle of Wight

I'm that little girl of ten again
In nineteen fifty-three
A wish of childhood now fulfilled
At Lee-on-Solent – by the sea

PICTURES OF JUSTICE

Now I'm just full of bright ideas
On how to pass the time
I saw this on the internet
So confess it isn't mine

To ring up random numbers
In countries, on the phone
And scare all their old ladies
In lockdown on their own

We'll say that we're from Microsoft
And their computer's on the blink
And rob them of their money
Before they've time to think

A fantasy – I'm dreaming
I wouldn't stoop to cause distress
To all the world's old ladies
While we're together in this mess

I'm not really horrid
Nor normally unkind
But what I'd do to scammers
Paints pictures in my mind

When with smarmy voices
They set out to target us
I summon up this image
Of them flattened by a bus

In centres dotted round the world
With scammers, caring not a jot
I'd line them up against the wall
And each one would be shot

I'd have gibbets up the high street
Hang them by their scrawny necks
'Cos they reduce old ladies
To nervous, frightened wrecks

They prey upon the elderly
The weak and old and frail
And I'd like to see the lot of them
Rot in the nearest jail

So when a scammer rings you up
Just terminate his call
He's a nasty little weevil
A brick short of a wall

Or string along his patter
But don't believe a word he said
Then tell him that the nurse has come
To put you back to bed

Be cautions and be wary
Don't think they've picked on you
We out there are many
And they're just an evil few

Don't get upset or worried
See the wheels of justice grind
Imagine their comeuppance
Paint the pictures in your mind

REFLECTION

There are roses on the table
Their fragrance fills the air
They're reflected in the mirror
But my image isn't there

Feather-light, a whispered breeze
A shadowed thought to share
Memories of those long gone
But my image isn't there

I see loved ones gathered
Hear the murmur of a prayer
Angel voices of the choir
But my image isn't there

Life reflected in the mirror
And into its gleam I stare
Believe me, I'm still with you
But my image isn't there

REMEMBER ME KINDLY

Remember me kindly
When I've turned to dust
Think of me gently
And grieve if you must
For I'll leave a footprint
A measure of worth
For the years of my living
Of my time spent on earth

So recall all the good days
The laughter we shared
And how I did love you
Always worried and cared
With each ray of sunshine
Every moonbeam above
Remember me kindly
And speak words of love

RIOTS 2020

Black man, white man, riots rage
Headlines on each tabloid page
Many injured, some lay dead
But whatever colour, their blood ran red

Now's not the time for angry deeds
Nor tension between race and creeds
Treat each person as your brother
If your cheek is slapped, then turn the other

All men are equal on this earth
Their race determined by their birth
Let's live in peace in this fair land
Side by side and hand in hand

SANITIZE

I've got a brand new perfume
Called Sanitizing Gel
I splash it on my pulse points
And behind my ears as well

I spray myself each morning
And ninety-nine percent
Of all the germs must perish
Though one lurks in the scent

So while the virus holds us hostage
Everyone must recognise
The power of soap and water
And the need to sanitize

SATURDAY NIGHT FEVER

July the fourth – our independence
They're opening up the pubs
The world and his wife will gather
In city centres and in clubs

But why pick on a Saturday
For an evening of high jinks
Distance rules all smothered
By alcoholic drinks

The police are all on standby
Expecting each and every lout
To disregard the danger
And the metre rule to flout

Much better would be Monday
A time that's dull and quiet
And not a day that's chosen
By the yobs to all run riot

But Saturday – I ask you
Stay indoors and drink your wine
And hope everyone is clobbered
If they cross the thin blue line

As politicians waffle
They do not seem to understand
Are their heads all buried
Like an ostrich in the sand

We don't want to be like Leicester
And see lockdown reinstated
Please don't act like total morons
Now the virus has abated

We all want to let our hair down
And no-one more than me
With a lifting of restrictions
In a life that's safe and free

SAVE THIS SINNER

Oh, dear Lord, in your mercy save me
From the lure of a Bassett's Jelly Baby
Let me shun all supermarket deals
On chocolate, sweets and Wagon Wheels
Please put my taste buds in denial
Lead me steadfast to the aisle
Where lettuce green and radish red
Will satisfy my needs instead

And, dear Lord, if it please your eyes
Let me reduce my thunder-thighs
Please curb my thirst when on a bender
And let my waist again be slender
And while you have it in your power
Please do not let me devour
Cake and biscuits, pizza, pies
And in your wisdom please devise
A single plan, a fool proof scheme
To give me a body sleek and lean

So hear my prayer and let me cease
Before I'm clinically obese
From all temptation save this sinner
McDonald fries and a chip-shop dinner
Just let me binge on leafy greens
And curly kale and runner beans
And, dear Lord, let me aspire
To evade the gluttony and desire
For puddings lashed with dairy cream
And let me focus on my dream
Don't see my hopes again be shelved
Let me fit my jeans, a perfect twelve

SEARCHING

Can a rose bloom in my heart once more
Can a thread of hope take form
Dear Lord, let me find comfort
And not feel the painful thorn

Please let the tears dry on my cheeks
Please let my spirits rise
And lift the cloak of black despair
Felt when a loved one dies

I'm searching for that glimmer
Of light, to move life on
So blinded by despondency
All joy of life has gone

Please let my searching find the path
Guide my footsteps slow but sure
Grant me peace and still my fears
Help me find an open door

And in the smile of loving faces
In the kindness of each deed
Let me feel the spark of life again
And thank those who plant the seed

SKY-BLUE-PINK

Brother, brother, have a drink with me
Whatever shade your skin might be
And when you bow your head in prayer
It doesn't matter what or where

In harmony a life we'll face
No matter what the creed or race
Come the day we'll not stop to think
Black or white or sky-blue-pink

SLIP UP

I have a lovely daughter
Who's kind as kind can be
And when we walk together
She takes great care of me

So walking through the mud, she said
"Be careful, Mum, don't slip
If you go down at your age
You could surely break a hip"

Well, one of us fell over
Sat down in mud and water
And, guess what, it wasn't me
It was my lovely daughter

SMILING STRANGER

Random acts of kindness
A smile, a door held open
A greeting from a stranger
Soft words so gently spoken

For those, the lost, the lonely
Who struggle through each day
That treasured friendly moment
Means more than words can say

Let's be that smiling stranger
Reach out with love and care
Those simple acts of kindness
Bring joy beyond compare

TAKE ME

Where have you been
Covid Nineteen
As still fit and well
Isolated I dwell
You just pass me by
Not a whisper or sigh
As I vegetate
In my bereaved state
Now my love is gone
Why must I carry on
With a life that is bare
And no-one to share
Let me give up this fight
Let your shadow alight
May others be free
Covid Nineteen
Take Me

TESTING TIME

First day back, I'm here in school
Observing the two metre rule
With distance markings round the blocks
As students sit 'A' level mocks
When masks hide smiles and eyes are wary
An alien concept some find scary
And as I invigilate each test
All spaced apart they do their best

With teacher care and school support
Exam room calm and no-one fraught
With no dramatics, each one steady
Revision done and all are ready
Instructions read and pens are poised
The room is hushed, no sound, no noise
And in my heart I wish them well
As I squirt the antiseptic gel

THE BEACON

The beacon's lit, it's shining
AstraZeneca's the name
And it will swing the balance
In the deadly Covid game

So roll your sleeves up ready
It's the beginning of the end
Be thankful for the vaccine
See our hearts and bodies mend

And let's thank all the scientists
The doctors, nurses, too
And in the words of Churchill
So many thank so few

TWILIGHT HOUR

In the silhouette of moonlight
Let the blossom's fragrance drift
As the world slips into silence
And peace is nature's gift

Let me sleep beneath a canopy
Of stars that brightly shine
Let me feel the breeze blow freshly
Smell the scent of forest pine

Let me slumber gently
When the twilight hour is through
Counting all my blessings
And the memories of you

TWILIGHT REBELLION

I'm tired of regulations
The restrictions and the rules
I'm sick of government advice
From hypocrites and fools

I survived the lonely lockdown
Isolated, on my own
Was banned from seeing loved ones
Made do with voices on the phone

Life is short, I'm in my dotage
No time to waste with fears
I won't give up my freedom
Let me enjoy my twilight years

So I'll not hide from the future
And while I'm hale and hearty
I'll throw precaution to the wind
And get out there and party

UNDER THE WIMPLE

It isn't much fun
To be novice or nun
But, oh, their life is so simple
On a bad hair-do day
They can hide it away
Under a stiffly starched wimple

What with poverty poor
And the chastity law
Life isn't their own, they can't grab it
On their knees every day
Assembled to pray
Their attributes under their habit

When their vows they take
To give up and forsake
All earthly pleasures and greed
No chocolate box choices
No children's raised voices
And men are an alien breed

So while we girls sit
And crochet and knit
And dream of our day of release
In isolation we be
But our hearts are free
Not chained like our sisters of peace

Yes, life is so simple
Under the wimple
And the habit shields all daily strife
As postulant or novice
You're called to high office
And serenely go forth as God's wife

VICTIM OF PRIVILEGE

Did you see the interview
The Oprah Winfrey show
The Whinger and her Ginger
Told us why they had to go

Oh how they must have suffered
With all that money there to oil
The obligation and the duty
That comes with being royal

If she had lived in Tudor times
The first Elizabeth would have said
'To The Tower, through Traitors Gate
And then chop off her head'

We weren't shown the lavish mansion
Swimming pool and all rich pickings
Just 'victimised' ex-royals
Feeding rescued chickens

But one thing to her credit
She's an actress sure and true
You could almost start believing
But we Brits – we see straight through

Now we've had all the dramatics
And from this sceptred isle we say
The monarchy won't miss you
Have a nice life in LA

VIRTUAL HUGS

I'm just a simple person
And, like you, I'm feeling glum
But there are people out there
Who are acting, oh, so dumb

They congregate in masses
In groups more than allowed
At least I'm sticking to the rules
And of that I can be proud

But I've seen the other nitwits
Acting like we're virus free
Disregarding safety measures
With the I.Q. of a pea

I may be old and grumpy
And although not paranoid
I'm following the guidelines
And crowds I will avoid

So to all the sheep and gormless
I won't mince my words
You won't help the situation
By gathering in herds

When I feel starved of comfort
I won't act like other mugs
I'll send greetings through the airwaves
And lots of virtual hugs

WAKES WEEK

It's Wakes Week up in Lancashire
In eighteen-ninety-five
The mill wheels have stopped turning
And Blackpool comes alive

The looms at last fall silent
As the shuttle ceases flight
And the spindle stops revolving
No more spinning from tonight

The cotton fluff will settle
The clamorous din will halt
The oily stench of weaving looms
To a standstill will be brought

The lads will court the lasses
Flat caps at jaunty angle
And with wages in their pockets
The pennies jingle-jangle

A donkey ride across the sands
And winkles picked with pin
Jellied eels and pie and mash
And coconuts to win

With Vaudeville at The Empire
Wonders every night performed
For just a brief time in the year
The toils of life transformed

Bread well spread with Shippam's paste
And many a lass would bake
To have with tea cold from a flask
A lump of lardy cake

To ride the tram along the front
And see the lights shine bright
To take the lift in Blackpool Tower
From the top a bonny sight

With toes dipped in the Irish Sea
Between The Ribble and The Wyre
See many a romance blossom
In that bright and breezy shire

For just a week or maybe two
A respite from daily grind
As the cotton mills fall silent
And all hardship's left behind

WANT OR NEED

Let's tighten belts together
And rid this world of greed
Forget about the things we want
And focus on the things we need

We don't need to get a take-away
Or flighty high-heeled shoes
Or buy music on the internet
To chase away our blues

We don't need crisps in packets
Ready meals or chocolate bars
We don't need all those fizzy drinks
Or great big fancy cars

We don't need jewels and handbags
Or gimmick gadgets round the home
We've a pleasant land to wander
And woodland paths to roam

Forget foie gras and caviar
Pick blackberries for free
And pour a nice strong cuppa
With beans on toast for tea

We don't need steak or salmon
Or oven chips when spuds will do
Just a loaf of bread – a pint of milk
And perhaps an egg or two

We don't need stylish hair-cuts
Or toenails painted pink
Be grateful we've got water
To run down our kitchen sink

In our society that's pampered
We waste more than we can eat
Think of those who have to struggle
Making do and both ends meet

Let's generate simplicity
Turn the heating down a notch
Don't heap the shopping trolley
And on expenditure keep watch

A deck-chair in the garden
No need to go abroad
Just close your eyes and dream awhile
When it's a trip you can't afford

So while Planet Earth lies bleeding
Let's sow a frugal seed
And remember all the millions
That our poor world has yet to feed

And before you spend your money
Ask a question of yourself
Do I need it or just want it
And leave it on the shelf

WASTED WORDS

I like to read my poetry
To those out there on Zoom
To bring my pearls of wisdom
Straight to their living room

So standing on my soapbox
Giving vent to whinge and whine
I admonished all the benders
Of the rules in lockdown time

Amongst us are the arrogant
To them rules don't apply
In pursuit of their own pleasures
While some fall sick and die

So my heartfelt plea coherent
All said in words that rhyme
We must not mix and mingle
'Til the bells of freedom chime

The audience applauded
Heads nodding – so astute
But sadly now I realise
My microphone's on mute

WE'LL MEET AGAIN

When Vera sang that famous song
Back in those war-time years
Not knowing we'd be singing it
To help us through Corona fears

'We'll Meet Again' she sang
'Don't know where, don't know when'
And now with families split apart
Just as we were back then

So as the country stands together
And again we fight a foe
No bombs to drop upon our heads
But courage we must show

And although the news is dismal
'We'll keep on smiling through'
Uniting our great nation
'Just as we always do'

As each day we fight the virus
Through uncertainty and pain
We'll lift our hearts together
'One sunny day we'll meet again'

As generations are divided
And families split apart
Until once more we meet again
Let love shine in your heart

Jean Hill